United States Presidents

Calvin Coolidge

Paul Joseph
ABDO Publishing Company

visit us at
www.abdopub.com

Published by Abdo Publishing Company 4940 Viking Drive, Edina, Minnesota 55435. Copyright © 1999 by Abdo Consulting Group, Inc. International copyrights reserved in all countries. No part of this book may be reproduced in any form without written permission from the publisher.

Printed in the United States.

Cover and Interior Photo credits: AP/Wide World, Archive, Corbis-Bettmann

Contributing editors: Robert Italia, Tamara L. Britton, K. M. Brielmaier
Book design/maps: Patrick Laurel

Library of Congress Cataloging-in-Publication Data

Joseph, Paul, 1970-
    Calvin Coolidge / Paul Joseph.
      p. cm. -- (United States presidents)
    Includes index.
    Summary: Discusses the personal life and political career of the man who became the thirtieth president of the United States in 1923 upon the death of President Harding.
    ISBN 1-57765-237-1
    1. Coolidge, Calvin, 1872-1933--Juvenile literature.
2. Presidents--United States--Biography--Juvenile literature.
[1. Coolidge, Calvin, 1872-1933. 2. Presidents.] I. Title.
II. Series: United States presidents (Edina, Minn.)
E792. J67   1999
973.91'5'092--dc21
[B]   98-16223
                                        CIP
                                        AC

Second printing 2002

Contents

Calvin Coolidge

*C*alvin Coolidge became president in 1923. The United States was doing well in the 1920s. Most people had good jobs. Families bought houses and cars. They made money on the **stock market**. Many Americans called these good times Coolidge Prosperity.

President Coolidge was praised for these good times. But then it all came crumbling down. And Coolidge was blamed. In 1929, the country's economy failed. This led to the **Great Depression**.

Coolidge was known as Silent Cal. He showed leadership not by talking but by doing. He believed in hard work.

Calvin Coolidge was not like most politicians. He rarely smiled. And he was quiet and shy. But people believed in his ideas.

Coolidge never lost a major election. He was a mayor, state senator, **lieutenant governor**, governor, vice president, and president. In every political office, Coolidge worked hard, was honest, and did what he thought was best for Americans.

A shocking event made Calvin Coolidge the thirtieth president of the United States. On August 3, 1923, he was awakened in the middle of the night. He was told that President Harding had died. Coolidge took the oath of office. Now he was the president of the United States.

Coolidge's journey to the White House was long. It started many years before on a Vermont farm.

President Calvin Coolidge

Calvin Coolidge (1872-1933)
Thirtieth President

BORN:	July 4, 1872
PLACE OF BIRTH:	Plymouth, Vermont
ANCESTRY:	English
FATHER:	John Calvin Coolidge (1845-1926)
MOTHER:	Victoria Josephine Moor Coolidge (1846-1885)
WIFE:	Grace Anna Goodhue (1879-1957)
CHILDREN:	Two boys
EDUCATION:	Plymouth District School; Black River Academy; St. Johnsbury Academy; Amherst College (1895)
RELIGION:	Congregationalist
OCCUPATION:	Lawyer
MILITARY SERVICE:	None
POLITICAL PARTY:	Republican

OFFICES HELD:	Member of Massachusetts legislature; mayor of Northampton, Massachusetts; member and president of Massachusetts senate; lieutenant governor of Massachusetts; governor of Massachusetts; vice president
AGE AT INAUGURATION:	51
YEARS SERVED:	1923-1925, 1925-1929
VICE PRESIDENT:	Charles G. Dawes (1925-1929)
DIED:	January 5, 1933, Northampton, Massachusetts, age 60
CAUSE OF DEATH:	Heart attack

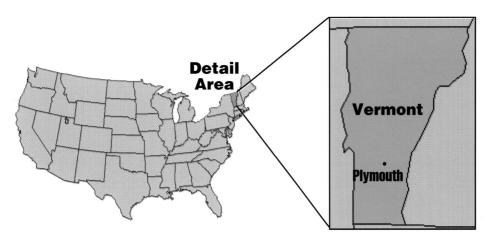

Birthplace of Calvin Coolidge

Young Calvin

*C*alvin Coolidge was born in Plymouth, Vermont, on July 4, 1872. He was the only son of John and Victoria Coolidge. They named him John Calvin after his father. But they called him Calvin to avoid confusion.

John was a farmer and a storekeeper. He also was active in local politics. Victoria was a quiet woman. She taught Calvin and his sister, Abbie, how to read and write.

Young Calvin helped his father on the farm. He drove the mowing machine, tended cattle, and planted potatoes. Calvin also had time to play and have fun.

In the winter, Calvin skated, sledded, and took hayrides. In the summer, Calvin loved to fish, swim, and ride horses. His sister was his closest friend. They spent much time together.

Seven-year-old Calvin Coolidge

Victoria became deathly ill when Calvin was only 12 years old. Calvin was very sad because he was close to her. After Victoria's death, Calvin's relationship with his father strengthened. This bond lasted throughout their lives.

Calvin went to Black River Academy in Ludlow, Vermont. He enjoyed school. He did well in every subject. Then his sister became ill.

No one knew what was wrong with Abbie. But it soon became clear she would die. Calvin was called home from school to be with her before she died. He was terribly saddened to lose another person to whom he was close.

Calvin Coolidge at Amherst College in 1895

In 1891, Calvin entered Amherst College in Massachusetts. He graduated with honors in 1895. He wanted to get involved in politics. Calvin decided the best way to begin was to become a lawyer.

Family and Politics

Coolidge studied law at a law firm in Northampton, Massachusetts. He became a lawyer in 1897. The next year, Coolidge took his first step in politics. That's when he was elected a Northampton city **councilman**.

Calvin Coolidge as a lawyer in 1905

In 1905, Coolidge married Grace Anna Goodhue. Grace was born in Burlington, Vermont, in 1879. She graduated from the University of Vermont in 1902. Then she taught at the Clarke Institute for the Deaf in Northampton.

Grace was the opposite of her shy and quiet husband. She was very warm and outgoing. But the couple had a wonderful and loving relationship. They had two sons. John was born in 1906. Calvin, Jr., was born in 1908.

In 1907, Coolidge was elected to the Massachusetts **House of Representatives**. There, he fought for women's and workers' rights. He reduced working hours. And he supported women's right to vote.

Coolidge wasn't like most politicians. He rarely smiled. And he didn't pat people on the back to get their votes. But he was honest, smart, and trustworthy. People liked Calvin Coolidge.

Coolidge was elected mayor of Northampton in 1910. He helped lower taxes. And he improved the fire and police departments.

Calvin and Grace Coolidge at the White House

In 1912, Coolidge was elected to the Massachusetts State Senate. Later, he became its president. There, he oversaw **committees.** And he helped resolve a mill strike.

In 1916, he was elected the **lieutenant governor** of Massachusetts. Coolidge kept fighting for workers' rights.

11

Governor Coolidge

*C*alvin Coolidge became governor of Massachusetts in 1918. Soon he was a national hero.

In 1919, the Boston police went on strike. There were two days of disorder. Then Coolidge called in the state guard to control the city.

Police Commissioner Edwin U. Curtis decided that the police had given up their jobs by going on strike. Labor leader Samuel Gompers wanted the strikers to get their jobs back. But Coolidge said no.

"There is no right to strike against the public safety by anybody, anywhere, anytime," Coolidge said. People across the country praised the governor for his tough stand.

In 1920, many **Republicans** wanted Calvin Coolidge to run for president. But Republican party leaders chose Warren G. Harding. Coolidge was picked to run for vice president.

The 1920 election marked the first time women could vote. Harding and Coolidge had always fought for women's rights. Women remembered this support and voted for them. This helped Harding and Coolidge win the race.

Governor Coolidge at the time he settled the Boston police strike

The Making of the Thirtieth United States President

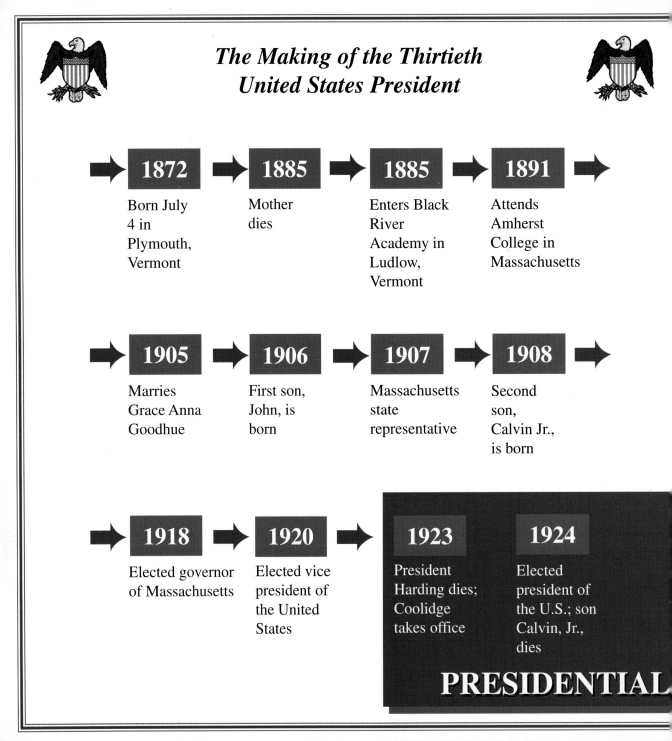

1872 → Born July 4 in Plymouth, Vermont

1885 → Mother dies

1885 → Enters Black River Academy in Ludlow, Vermont

1891 → Attends Amherst College in Massachusetts

1905 → Marries Grace Anna Goodhue

1906 → First son, John, is born

1907 → Massachusetts state representative

1908 → Second son, Calvin Jr., is born

1918 → Elected governor of Massachusetts

1920 → Elected vice president of the United States

1923 President Harding dies; Coolidge takes office

1924 Elected president of the U.S.; son Calvin, Jr., dies

PRESIDENTIAL

Calvin Coolidge

"The business of America is business."

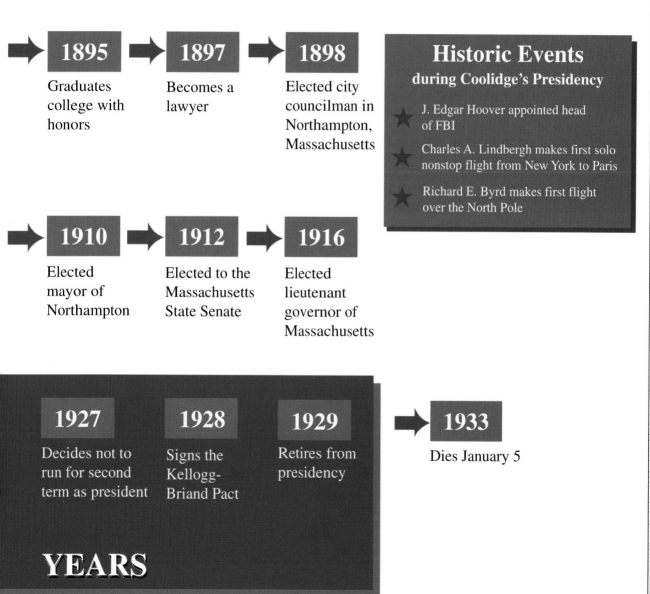

1895
Graduates college with honors

1897
Becomes a lawyer

1898
Elected city councilman in Northampton, Massachusetts

Historic Events
during Coolidge's Presidency

★ J. Edgar Hoover appointed head of FBI

★ Charles A. Lindbergh makes first solo nonstop flight from New York to Paris

★ Richard E. Byrd makes first flight over the North Pole

1910
Elected mayor of Northampton

1912
Elected to the Massachusetts State Senate

1916
Elected lieutenant governor of Massachusetts

1927
Decides not to run for second term as president

1928
Signs the Kellogg-Briand Pact

1929
Retires from presidency

1933
Dies January 5

YEARS

The President At Work

*P*resident Coolidge cleaned up his **administration**. He hired two lawyers. They brought to court anyone involved in political crimes.

*Interior Secretary
Albert B. Fall*

The most famous of these crimes was the Teapot Dome Scandal. It was named for government land in Wyoming. **Secretary of the Interior** Albert B. Fall had allowed oil companies to drill on Teapot Dome. But first, they had to give him money. Fall was sent to prison for taking **bribes**.

Americans liked President Coolidge's swift action and firm leadership. He restored the country's trust in government. Coolidge continued to keep taxes and government spending low. And he kept government from interfering with businesses.

In 1924, 16-year-old Calvin, Jr., was playing tennis at the White House. He got a blister on his foot. It became **infected**, and he died within a few days.

Coolidge suffered from this new loss. He had less and less energy for politics. Later, he said that with his son's death "went the power and the glory of the presidency."

Coolidge with his wife, Grace, and two sons, John (left) and Calvin, Jr.

Coolidge was tired and sad. But he stayed in the 1924 election for president. Coolidge won easily.

President Coolidge kept his firm stand against taxes and spending. Businesses continued to grow. But individuals did not receive favors.

Congress tried twice to pass the McNary-Haugen bill. This bill would help farmers get out of **debt**. But Coolidge stopped the bill both times. Though he had been a farmer, Coolidge thought people should not receive government handouts.

In 1928, Coolidge supported the Kellogg-Briand Pact. This agreement outlawed the use of war to settle quarrels between countries. Sixty-two nations signed the treaty. **Secretary of State** Frank B. Kellogg wrote it. For his efforts, Kellogg won the **Nobel Peace Prize**.

Opposite page:
Calvin Coolidge's
1925 inauguration

The Seven "Hats" of the U.S. President

A president can serve only two terms. Each term lasts four years. When Coolidge was president, this law did not exist.

A president is elected or re-elected every four years.

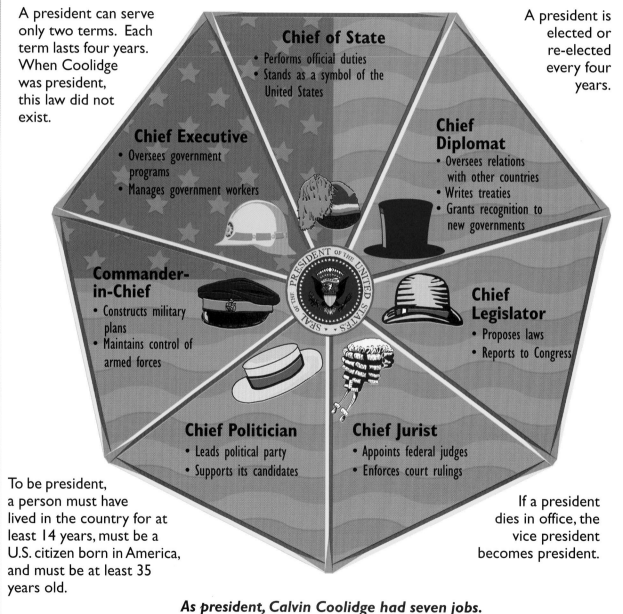

Chief of State
- Performs official duties
- Stands as a symbol of the United States

Chief Executive
- Oversees government programs
- Manages government workers

Chief Diplomat
- Oversees relations with other countries
- Writes treaties
- Grants recognition to new governments

Commander-in-Chief
- Constructs military plans
- Maintains control of armed forces

Chief Legislator
- Proposes laws
- Reports to Congress

Chief Politician
- Leads political party
- Supports its candidates

Chief Jurist
- Appoints federal judges
- Enforces court rulings

SEAL OF THE PRESIDENT OF THE UNITED STATES

To be president, a person must have lived in the country for at least 14 years, must be a U.S. citizen born in America, and must be at least 35 years old.

If a president dies in office, the vice president becomes president.

As president, Calvin Coolidge had seven jobs.

The Three Branches of the U.S. Government

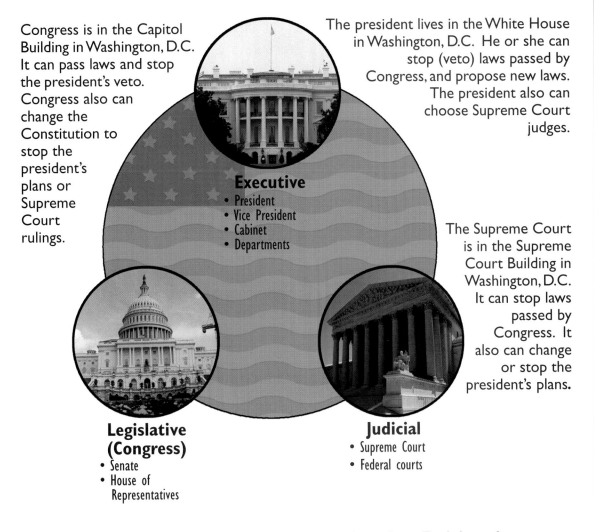

Congress is in the Capitol Building in Washington, D.C. It can pass laws and stop the president's veto. Congress also can change the Constitution to stop the president's plans or Supreme Court rulings.

The president lives in the White House in Washington, D.C. He or she can stop (veto) laws passed by Congress, and propose new laws. The president also can choose Supreme Court judges.

Executive
- President
- Vice President
- Cabinet
- Departments

The Supreme Court is in the Supreme Court Building in Washington, D.C. It can stop laws passed by Congress. It also can change or stop the president's plans.

Legislative (Congress)
- Senate
- House of Representatives

Judicial
- Supreme Court
- Federal courts

The U.S. Constitution formed three government branches. Each branch has power over the others. So, no single group or person can control the country. The Constitution calls this "separation of powers."

Coolidge Prosperity

*U*nder President Coolidge's leadership, America did better than ever. Big businesses like mining and banking became bigger. Stores spread across the country. Factories shipped huge amounts of goods.

People bought houses and cars. They made money on the **stock market**. Workers enjoyed better pay and a shorter work week. Some even got paid vacations and free medical care. These were things that had never been given before. Coolidge Prosperity gave Americans a better life.

Opposite page:
Coolidge goes fishing
in Vermont

Coolidge Goes Home

*I*n 1927, President Coolidge put out a historic statement. He said, "I do not choose to run for president in 1928." The nation was stunned. Times were good. Why wouldn't he want to be re-elected? Coolidge did not explain his decision.

The **Republicans** chose Herbert Hoover to run for president. Hoover won the election easily.

In March 1929, Coolidge returned to Northampton. There, he spent time with his family. He also wrote magazine and newspaper articles. And he wrote a book.

In October 1929, the good times came to a crashing end. Too much spending and money lending in the 1920s led to the **Great Depression**. Stock prices dropped, banks closed, and businesses failed. Worst of all, many Americans lost their jobs.

Coolidge was saddened. Most citizens felt that his leadership had failed. The same people who once praised him were now blaming him for America's troubles.

On January 5, 1933, Coolidge suffered a fatal heart attack at home. He was only 60 years old. Coolidge was buried in Plymouth, Vermont in the same cemetery as his father and son.

True to his nature, Calvin Coolidge has the simplest grave marker of any U.S. president. It reads: "Calvin Coolidge: July 4, 1872 - January 5, 1933."

Police on horseback watch the nervous crowds outside the New York Stock Exchange building. The stock market crash of 1929 has begun.

Fun Facts

- President Coolidge loved to sit on the White House porch, rock in his chair, and play the harmonica. He finally had to stop because large crowds gathered to listen.

- President Coolidge hated to waste time. His first **cabinet** meeting lasted only 15 minutes. Most cabinet meetings last many hours.

- Coolidge thought that people talked too much. He liked to sit and observe without having to speak. One night at a dinner party, a woman bet Coolidge that she could make him say three words. Coolidge stared at her and finally said, "You lose."

- President Coolidge never wasted a penny. White House guests were served water in paper cups, and small portions at dinner. Coolidge even tried to raise chickens in the White

House yard because it would be cheaper than buying them—
but they didn't taste good.

- President Coolidge loved animals. He had many pets,
  including dogs, cats, and a raccoon that he walked on
  a leash!

Former President Coolidge on his farm

Glossary

administration - the people in charge of running the government.

bribe - anything given to someone so they will do something wrong.

cabinet - a group of advisers chosen by the president.

committee - a group of people chosen to do some special thing.

Congress - the lawmaking body of a nation. It is made up of the House of Representatives and the Senate.

councilman - an elected official who makes laws for and manages a city.

debate - a public talk about topics or questions.

debt - something owed to someone.

Great Depression - the failure of the U.S. economy starting in 1929 and lasting through the 1930s. A depression is a time when business is slow and people are out of work.

House of Representatives - a group of people who are elected by citizens to represent them. They meet in Washington, D.C., and make laws for the nation. Each state also has a House of Representatives to make state laws.

infect - to bring disease into the body through contact with germs.

lieutenant governor - an elected state official who ranks below governor.

Nobel Peace Prize - a prize given each year to a person who works for world peace.

notary public - a person who can witness documents and official events.

Republican - one of two main political parties in the United States today. Republicans are often conservative and believe in less government.

secretary of the interior - an adviser to the president who handles the country's natural resources.

secretary of state - an adviser to the president who handles problems with other countries.

stock market - a place where stocks and bonds, which represent parts of businesses, are bought and sold.

Internet Sites

Calvin Coolidge Memorial Web Site
http://www.calvin-coolidge.org/
Visit the Web site dedicated to the legacy of the 30th president, Calvin Coolidge. This site has an extensive biography on Coolidge along with his speeches, cabinet, and photos.

Welcome to the White House
http://www.whitehouse.gov
The official Web site of the White House. After an introduction from the current president of the United States, the site takes you through biographies of each president. Get information on White House history, art in the White House, first ladies, first families, and much more.

POTUS—Presidents of the United States
http://www.ipl.org/ref/POTUS/
In this Web site you will find background information, election results, cabinet members, presidency highlights, and some odd facts on each of the presidents. Links to biographies, historical documents, audio and video files, and other presidential sites are also included to enrich this site.

These sites are subject to change. Go to your favorite search engine and type in United States presidents for more sites.

Pass It On

History enthusiasts: educate readers around the country by passing on information you've learned about presidents or other important people who have changed history. Share your little-known facts and interesting stories. We want to hear from you!

To get posted on the ABDO Publishing Company Web site, email us at "History@abdopub.com"
Visit the ABDO Publishing Company Web site at www.abdopub.com

Index